· Scott Washburn ·

THE BEST BEAR HUGS EVER

Illustrated by Laura Liberatore
Original music composed by Lucas Denzer

A Sensible Knowledge Book

A Sensible Knowledge Book
Published by Sensible Knowledge
© 2012 by Scott Washburn
Second printing, 2019

Publisher's Cataloging-in-Publication
(Provided by Quality Books, Inc.)

Washburn, Scott.
  The best bear hugs ever / author, Scott Washburn ;
illustrated by Laura Liberatore ; original music
composed by Lucas Denzer.
    p. cm.
  SUMMARY: A parent visits the zoo and hugs baby
elephants, monkeys, tigers, giraffes, and bears looking
for the best bear hug ever. The parent finds the best
bear hug when he returns home and his baby runs to him
with open arms. Includes music notation of a short
lullaby. Pictorially portrays baby with hearing disability.
  Audience: Ages 0-6.
  ISBN 978-0-9855145-1-8
  ISBN 978-0-9855145-2-5

  1. Hugging--Juvenile fiction. 2. Parent and child--
Juvenile fiction. [1. Hugging--Fiction. 2. Animals--
Fiction.] I. Liberatore, Laura, ill. II. Denzer,
Lucas. III. Title.

  PZ7.W2584Bes 2012   [E]
                  QBI12-600173

Printed and bound in China
Production Date: August 2019
Plant & Location: Printed by Everbest Printing (Guangzhou, China), Co. Ltd
Job / Batch #: 80053

Look us up to find more about the creators behind
The Best Bear Hugs Ever.

Scott Washburn
www.TheBestBearHugsEver.com
www.facebook.com/TBBHE

Illustrated by Laura Liberatore
liberatorelaura.wixsite.com/lauraliberatore

Original Music composed by Lucas Denzer
www.LucasDenzer.com

Special Thanks

To my wife, for all the sacrifices she makes for our
family, and for her love that warms all our hearts.
To my kids, for being the inspiration behind
The Best Bear Hugs Ever.

To my parents, for all the years of love and support.
To my good friends who have helped with this story-
May good friends stay close no matter how far apart.
To my children's teachers for their input on this story
and for their dedication to helping our children's future.

On a bright, sunny day, in search of the best bear hugs ever, I walked to the zoo. I wanted to see the bears to experience the best bear hugs ever.

On my way to the bears, I saw a large gray animal with great big ears and a long trunk.

Elephants!

I told Mother Elephant I was on my way to see the bears for the best bear hugs ever.

Mother Elephant said, "You don't need to see the bears for that. My Baby Elephant gives the best bear hugs ever. This I will never forget."

"Really?" I asked. "Can I hug Baby Elephant?"

"Yes, you can," said Mother Elephant.

So, I hugged Baby Elephant. The hug was warm and scratchy. Baby Elephant did not give the best bear hugs ever. Something was missing. So, I continued to walk toward the bears.

On my way to the bears, I saw a brown animal with long arms and a long tail swinging in a tree.

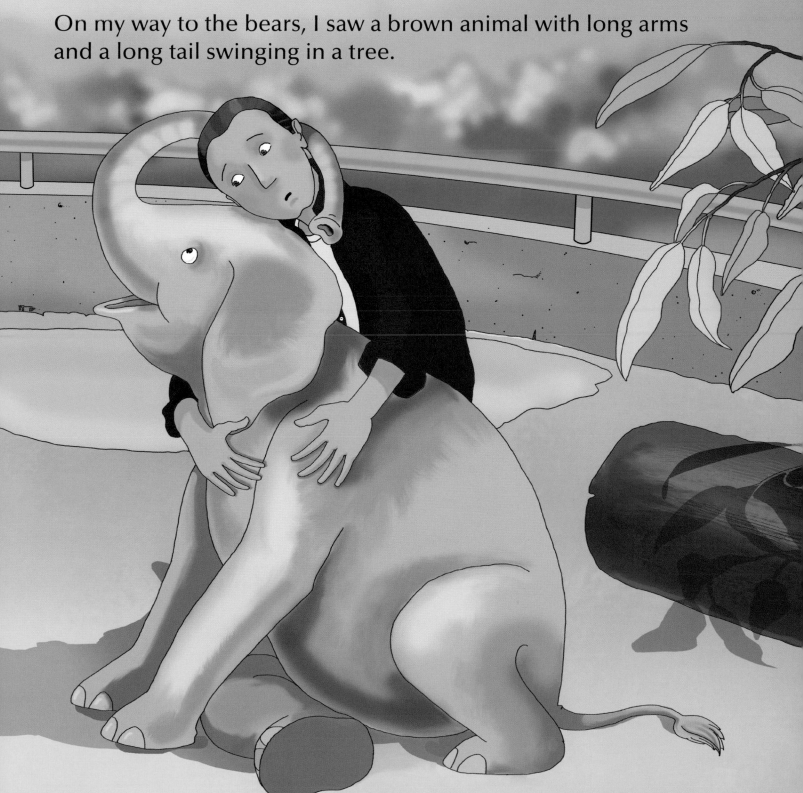

Monkeys!

I told Mother Monkey I was on my way to see the bears for the best bear hugs ever.

Mother Monkey said, "You don't need to see the bears for that. My Baby Monkey gives the best bear hugs ever."

"Really?" I asked. "Can I hug Baby Monkey?"

"Yes, you can," said Mother Monkey.

So, I hugged Baby Monkey. The hug was soft. The hug was also messy. Baby Monkey did not give the best bear hugs ever. Something was missing. So, I continued to walk toward the bears.

On my way to the bears, I saw an orange and black striped animal that looked like a huge cat.

Tigers!

I told Mother Tiger I was on my way to see the bears for the best bear hugs ever.

Mother Tiger said, "You don't need to see the bears for that. My Baby Tiger gives the best bear hugs ever."

"**R**eally?" I asked. "Can I hug Baby Tiger?"
"Yes, you can," said Mother Tiger.

So, I hugged Baby Tiger. The hug was warm. The hug also tickled. But Baby Tiger did not give the best bear hugs ever. Something was missing. So, I continued to walk toward the bears.

On my way to the bears, I saw a giant animal with towering legs and a long, long neck.

Giraffes!

I told Mother Giraffe I was on my way to see the bears for the best bear hugs ever.

Mother Giraffe said, "You don't need to see the bears for that. My Baby Giraffe gives the best bear hugs ever."

"Really?" I asked. "Can I hug Baby Giraffe?"

"Yes, you can," said Mother Giraffe.

So, I hugged Baby Giraffe. The hug was soft. The hug was also slimy. Baby Giraffe did not give the best bear hugs ever. Something was missing. So, I continued to walk toward the bears.

Just past the giraffes, there was a big brown furry animal with a short stubby tail.

Bears!

Three bears - Father Bear, Mother Bear, and Baby Bear.

Finally!

"I am looking for the best bear hugs ever," I said to the bears.

Father Bear and Mother Bear smiled at each other. Mother Bear said to me, "We are bears, and our Baby Bear gives the best bear hugs ever."

I was excited. I asked Mother and Father Bear if I could hug Baby Bear.

"Yes, of course you can. See why they call it a 'bear hug,'" said Mother Bear.

Finally, I would be able to experience the best bear hugs ever!

I reached in to give Baby Bear a hug, and Baby Bear reached in to give me a hug. The hug was warm. The hug was soft. The hug was also wet.

I knew right away that Baby Bear did not give the best bear hugs ever. Something was missing. It was getting late, so I decided to walk back home.

Sadly, I walked back home, past the bears, the giraffes, the tigers, the monkeys, and the elephants. I did not find the best bear hugs ever, because something was always missing. I wondered if I would eventually find the best bear hugs ever.

Back at home, I opened the front door.

There you were. You saw me walk into the room and started running toward me.

I leaned down to welcome your opening arms.

You gave me a hug that was so warm, so soft, and so full of love. Right there and then I realized my baby gives the best bear hugs ever. This I will never forget!

The Best Bear Hugs Ever

Words By: Scott Washburn
Music By: Lucas Denzer

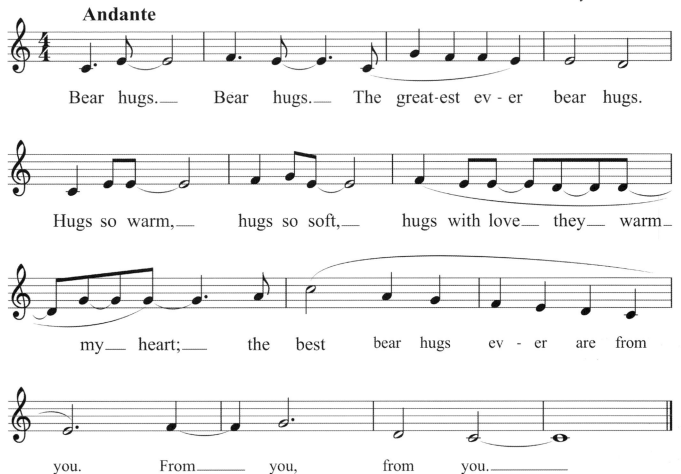

Andante

Bear hugs.___ Bear hugs.___ The great-est ev - er bear hugs.

Hugs so warm,___ hugs so soft,___ hugs with love___ they___ warm___

my___ heart;___ the best bear hugs ev - er are from

you. From___ you, from you.___

CERTIFICATE OF RECOGNITION

Awarded to

_____

For Giving

THE BEST BEAR HUGS EVER

On this _____ day of _____ _____

_____

SIGNATURE

www.TheBestBearHugsEver.com